The Sassy Way

to

STARTING

a

SUCCESSFUL BLOG

when you have

NO CLUE!

7 Steps to WordPress Bliss…

by G. Gabrielle

Third Edition Paperback: July 2018

ISBN-13: 978-1519146120
ISBN-10: 1519146124

The Cataloging-In-Publication Data is on file with the Library of Congress.

This is a **SassyZenGirl** *Guide*

TABLE OF CONTENTS

Please Bookmark the RESOURCES PAGE
so you can access all tools and resources mentioned
throughout this book with direct links to each:

SassyZenGirl.com/Blog-Resources

Introduction

You have some great ideas, but no audience to share them with.

Tech stuff scares you, and building your own website seems as impossible as climbing Mount Everest.

People have told you to start a blog. And you have many great ideas. You *love* writing.

You also heard how much money successful bloggers make. And the awesome number of people they can reach around the world.

Sounds intriguing. Fascinating really. Definitely something you would like to try, but you don't know how, and all that tech stuff scares you.

And......you don't have thousands of dollars to spend on a web designer. If you start a blog, you have to do it yourself.

Catch 22?

Not really! If any of the above rings true, you have come to the right place.

You will find that starting a blog is surprisingly easy - and inexpensive! - and really doesn't require any tech skills.

So take a deep breath, grab a coffee, and enjoy the ride!

Who Am I?

Well....I tell you who I am not... :) - a super-duper hi-tech web geek who can't relate to newbies with no prior tech skills or experience.

My background is in music. For many years I toured as a conductor and pianist/organist, playing Carnegie Hall and other "cool" venues, even performing for the Pope. I ran a successful music company and figured out how to fill large concert halls without a massive marketing budget (even before I knew anything about online marketing). I also used my company as a social entrepreneur to raise funds about $30K for *Doctors Without Borders*.

Four years ago I took a break from this exhilarating, yet exhausting life and started traveling, mostly road tripping all over the US and now around the world.

I discovered blogging and writing as a wonderful new creative expression, and after publishing my first book and writing a little amateur blog for a while, decided to up my game and study with the top guns in the blogging world.

Within 2 years, my blog grew to a large international following and my books got me onto the coveted **Top 100 Business Author** list where I outranked such greats as Brian Tracy, Robert Kiyosaki and Russell Brunson.

Everything I have learned is condensed into this little book to help you get started with a cool blog the smart way. And without reading tedious manuals or pulling your hair.

I remember how overwhelming it was when I first started - especially all those tech words - and I want to spare you some of the frustrations and beginner's mistakes that I made.

I will break it down step by step. Explain every funky word, so you don't have to google it (as I had to... frequently) - and share some tools that worked for me.

Initially, there will be a small learning curve like with anything new. Don't be discouraged if - on occasion - something may seem difficult or you can't figure it out. Sometimes, stepping away and coming back the next day is all you need (or a walk with your dog...;-)

Steady does it, and if you keep at it - step by step - you will find that within a short time things will become a lot easier, and you will actually enjoy working on your blog.

Most of all, never forget WHY you are doing it. You obviously have something wonderful to share with the world, and you are passionate about it. Keeping that in mind will get you passed the few blocks you might encounter along the way. At any time, if you have questions or feel stuck, feel free to ask in our supportive Facebook Group: **SassyZenGirl.Group**

And …… don't forget to share a link to your new blog with us once it's up and running. We can't wait to see your new masterpiece and share in the excitement… :)

Sound good? - then let's get started!

How this book works:

This guide is divided into 3 parts:

Part I: Basic Set-up of your Site - *STEP 1-3*

Covers all the technical aspects of getting your blog up and running.

STEP #1: Web Software - What is WordPress and why do most successful bloggers use it?

STEP #2: Hosting - Finding a good home base for your blog

STEP #3: Creating your Brand - Choosing and registering your domain name

Part II: Designing your Site - *STEP 4-6*

This is where the fun begins! - Taking the basic structure and turning it into a great looking, highly functional site.

STEP #4: WordPress Set up - A first look at your site & features

STEP #5: Pick a Theme - Styling your site to awesomeness

STEP #6: Plugins, Mailing Lists & Google Analytics - Turning your blog into a performance ninja

Part III: Making your Blog Successful - *STEP 7*

A massive resource chapter with some of the best (and mostly free) blogging & marketing training available.

STEP #7: Blogging & Marketing Training - Learning from the MASTERS

Instead of reinventing the wheel, learn from the best and save yourself years of struggle and frustration.

Step #1: Web Software

What is *WordPress* and why do most successful bloggers use it?

If you are interested in blogging, then you have probably heard about *WordPress* and might be wondering what all the fuss is about.

Well….quite simply, *WordPress* is the website software that most blogs operate on.

First released in 2003, it quickly became a worldwide phenomenon, powering more than 70 million websites today.

Wordpress is not just a blogging tool though, but is also well-suited to build highly flexible, feature rich websites. And it is VERY easy to use, requiring no knowledge of complex codes, html, or the like.

If you are comfy with *Microsoft Word*, handling *WordPress* will be a breeze. It uses a similar editor to format pages and you can design and update your site without spending hundreds or thousands of dollars on a professional designer.

Even better, it is completely FREE, because *WordPress* is an "open source project," meaning hundreds of volunteers from all around the world are constantly evolving and improving code and features.

There are thousands of "plugins", "widgets" and "themes".....

Say what....?

Yep... that's exactly how *I* felt in the beginning, but all those funky words will be explained in the coming chapters, not to worry....

In addition, "*WordPress* is made to do SEO well" to quote Matt Cutts from *Google*. "SEO" stands for "Search Engine Optimization". Those are the tools and techniques that help your blog rank high on Google and other search engines, so people can find you easily.

If you are looking for a simple tool to build your site without any tech knowledge — no other system is this easy!

Wordpress is a NON profit platform using the extension Wordpress.ORG.

An important distinction to *commercial* platforms like Wordpress.COM, Weebly, Wix, etc.

Rookie Mistake Alert:

Please read the following carefully as this is one of the most common rookie mistakes, and it's easy to get confused at first:

Commercial platforms usually start with free versions and it all looks so simple and practical, but - if you want to have full functionality - and your own domain name - meaning, not something ugly and unprofessional like:

   yoursite.blogspot.com   or   *yoursite.wordpress.com*

you have to pay a monthly fee.

In addition - and this is really important to understand - commercial platforms *own* your site and control your content.

You didn't know that, right?

They can shut you down and change the rules at any time.

Worse, - and this is huge(!) - you can only use THEIR small array of apps and tools, which is very limiting.

In fact, most of the thousands of *amazing* (mostly free) apps ("plugins", "widgets") offered by Wordpress.org, will not be available to you on commercial platforms.

Wha…??!!!

Yep, that's right.

You get the amateur-kiddie version and then they even make a profit off your site.

If that wasn't bad enough, commercial platforms will often charge a commission once you start using a shopping cart or sell products, which you probably will at some point.

So… in case it hasn't sunk in…

Commercial platforms are <u>built to make a profit off YOUR site</u>!

They make the rules, they can change them whenever they want to and then you are stuck and have to comply.

Similar to renting an apartment and being at the whim of a landlord vs. owning your own house and being in complete control.

Obviously, you should *own* your website or blog, so commercial platforms are an absolute no-go!

Instead, what you need is your own, "self-hosted" website using the FREE software Wordpress.ORG.

To quote Blogger and Bestselling Author Rembert N Parker:

"Not knowing any better, I set my blog up on Wordpress.com instead of installing Wordpress on a self-hosted website. I cannot emphasize enough <u>how much</u> of a mistake that was!

In theory, you can now upgrade Wordpress.com sites for a fee (initially $250) so you can upload many of the unavailable features of Wordpress.org, but it is far better to avoid that site altogether and start with Wordpress on a self-hosted site."

What the booty is "Hosting"?

Simply put, a hosting company is the home base for your blog. It "stores" your blog's data - all the pages, design, files, archives, etc., - and also functions as a "broadcasting station" to beam all your awesome content into cyberspace.

Blogger, Weebly, Wix and co., are hosting your site and that is where the problem lies. That's what gives them complete control.

Instead, you can outsource hosting to an independent hosting company and then use the free Wordpress software to build your site (don't worry - really easy!).

THAT will give you freedom, control and access to thousands of fantastic (mostly free) apps and tools. The best the internet has to offer!

That's the way to build a successful blogging platform and/or business!

Make sense?

The final massive benefit of Wordpress - and the one you will love the most…:) - is that it's extremely easy to use and requires no tech or coding knowledge whatsoever.

How awesome is that?

Like I said, it's very similar to using Microsoft Word, very similar editor, and I'll show you exactly what to do in the next chapters.

Ready?

Cool. Let's roll!

Step #2: Hosting

Finding a good home base for your blog

Now, let's find a good home base for your blog!

In the last chapter I explained what "hosting" is. In this chapter we will quickly cover what to consider when choosing a good hosting company. *(I know, seems boring, but is actually quite interesting....:)*

Let's start with a list of Top 10 Factors that make for good, reliable web hosting. It's good to know these terms and what they mean.

Then I will share one awesome example that has worked really well for me (after some rather bad experiences initially). Plus, a *special 50% discount* that I negotiated for *SassyZenGirl* readers, so you can get started with one of the top services in the business without paying a fortune.

Excited?

Then here we go (short 'n sweet):

The 10 Important Factors when selecting a Web Hosting Service

1) Good Uptime/Reliable Servers: should be 99%
This is super important and ensures that your website will always be up and running. Cheap companies often have server downtimes, meaning your website will be down, no one can find it - sometimes for hours or days at a time...

2) Free SSL Certificate
*An SSL Certificate makes your site a lot more secure and protects from hackers. It is mandatory if you accept credit cards on your site, but even without payment features, Google now favors sites with SSL, because they seem more legitimate and you get an additional SEO benefit (SEO = how you rank high in Google, so people can find your site when they "google" - if SEO is new to you, **my pink Beginner SEO Guide** will get you started quickly and painlessly...:)*

3) Free One-Click WordPress Installer
Should be easy to set up and not take more than a minute. Any good hosting company should have this!

4) Unlimited Disk Space and Bandwidth

Unless you suddenly get something like 100,000 daily visitors to your site (unlikely in the beginning), you should have no limitations in your usage.

5) Free Backups

You should still have your own backup program (will be discussed in the plugin chapter), but your hosting company should also backup everything - and for free, of course

6) Free Site Transfers

If you already have a site and want to transfer it to a new hosting company at a better rate/conditions, your new hosting company should do this for free.

7) Top Notch Tech Support

Minimal wait times for online chat or phone support

8) Money Back Guarantee of *at least* 30 Days

9) Low Price = less than $5 per month

for 1-2 sites you should not pay more than $5/month. Be careful though with $1-2 hosting sites. Their quality is usually bad, lots of downtime, no customer support etc - and google often considers them spammy and occasionally bans all sites hosted there.....

10) Good Reviews from reputable Review sites

✻✻✻✻✻✻✻✻

Now that you know what to look for, you can start researching online. As promised, here is my top web hosting choice - where I host all my sites: **Inmotion Hosting.**

TThey check out on all 10 Points - incl. a free SSD drive and a 90 day money back guarantee - and are awarded year after year:

"Best Web Hosting Company"
"Best Web Hosting for WordPress"
"Best Web Hosting for Small Business"

by the top review sites, plus an A+ rating with the Better Business Bureau.

Even better, the special link includes a **FREE Premium Website Builder** with 200+ premium page templates that will make designing an awesome looking website so much easier - even as a total beginner!

This link will give you the 50% discount I promised, reducing the price to just 3.99 per month for **2** sites! - Yep, that's right! - you can even share the cost with a friend and get their site hosted as well:

SassyZenGirl.com/Web-Hosting

Keep that window open. We'll return to it in a few minutes, after we go over choosing and registering a name for your blog (your "domain" name)…

Step #3: Creating your Brand

Choosing and registering a domain name

This is an exciting part of the process: finding a cool name for your blog or business.

It will become your online identity for years to come and define your blog and what you stand for, well beyond just cyberspace.

You probably played with a few ideas and asked your friends for feedback. And maybe you already found an awesome name for your blog, one that you are really excited about.

There are, however, a few more factors to consider when choosing a domain name - your brand name - including whether it is marketable and user-friendly.

If you can't think of a good name, but have a few keywords that you would like to include, these tools can help:

NameBoy.com

Dotomator.com

Bustaname.com

Next, you need to check whether your dream name is still available. These are the three best-known domain name registrars and you can quickly check there:

NameCheap.com

GoDaddy.com

Name.com

I have all my domain names stored with Namecheap, because their prices are great (around $10 for most domains), they don't pester you with a million upsells like GoDaddy during checkout, and - VERY importantly - they include **free Domain Privacy/ Whois Registration**, which you definitely want (or get bombarded with daily spam mail).

Whichever you choose, make sure that "privacy protection" is checked, so your info is not publicly available.

If your dream name is not available, you might find a variation that works, keeping in mind the .com and 'dash' rules described in the free report.

If you can't make a final decision yet, don't let that stop you. Just pick an interim name so you can sign up for hosting and start building your site.

Once you settle on a final name, you simply register it, and "point" the old name to the new (super-easy to do - your hosting company will help you with that at no extra cost).

Now, let's get you set up!

Setting up Hosting

First, go back to the ***InMotion* discount link** from the last chapter.

You should arrive at this screen:

Once you are on the correct page, click on **Get Started** and then the **Launch** option (left column):

The *Launch* option offers up to two websites per account, and that is usually enough. You can always upgrade later or choose a different option if you need hosting for more than two sites.

Next, choose 12 or 24 months. The price will go up slightly for the shorter version, so I usually choose 24 months, because you want to lock in the 50% discount for as long as possible. With web hosting companies, you always pay annually or bi-annually. That's how you get great deals and then you don't have to worry about paying for hosting again for the next 2 years.

On the next page, choose the location nearest to you and decline a dedicated IP address:

Scrolling down, decline the design offer, BUT choose the free installation of Wordpress:

Click **continue** and enter your chosen domain name.

If you don't have a domain name yet, it will be cheaper to buy one from **NameCheap.com(*)**, plus they include free Domain privacy/Whois registration, which you definitely want that (or get bombarded with daily spam mail). Once you registered your domain with Namecheap, come back and enter it here.

On the next screen, enter your email address.

And then your account, billing and payment information. After that, you can review everything and then click **purchase**. You are now paid up for the next 1-2 years of hosting!

Next, you will receive a welcome email with your login info and the option to set up a password.

Open the email and first, scroll ALL the way down. You will find the following *WordPress* login information, specific to your account:

1) wp-admin link
2) user name
3) password

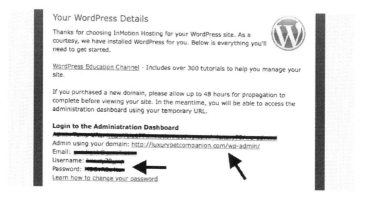

Save that info for later. You will need it in the next chapter to log into your *WordPress* account.

Next, scroll back to the beginning of the email and click on the red link that says: ***"To get started, set your password here"***.

This will get you logged into *InMotion's* admin area.

Please note, that you just received TWO different logins:

TOP of the email:

login for your **hosting account** (in this case, *InMotion*). Here, you will manage your domains, email accounts, and other tech set up for your website.

Don't worry, you won't spend much time there, and the few things you need can easily be handled by tech support in just a few minutes.

BOTTOM of the email:

login for your *WordPress* **account**, the one I asked you to save. *WordPress* is the web software that will allow you to *design* your website. It will become clearer in the next chapter, but just as a little heads-up.

Inside your Hosting account *(login info from* TOP *of the email)* click on:

My Account -> Manage My Account

and you will see the following screen:

Don't worry about all the different icons for now. The most important feature will be your **cPanel** (left arrow). That's the area where the technical management of your websites and hosting takes place (NOT the design - that happens within *WordPress* and we'll go there in just a few moments).

Let's have a look:

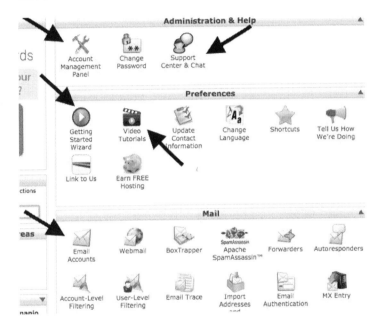

I marked some of the more important features to help you get oriented. The **Getting Started Wizard** and **Video Tutorials** are very helpful. Short 'n sweet and easy-to-follow. You can also use them later to set up your email accounts once your site and contact form are set up.

Two additional areas that you will occasionally use are

Domains: To add a new domain use **Addon Domains**.

To "point" and old domain to the new use **Redirects**.

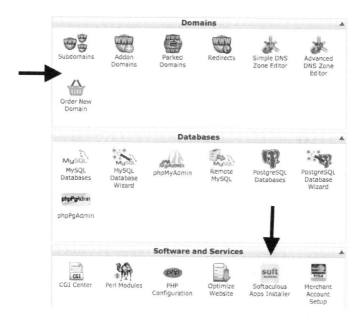

Software and Services: options like **Softaculous** (to install apps like *WordPress*) and **Merchant Accounts**

This also goes for changing *Nameservers* if you purchased your domain with a registrar like *NameCheap* or *GoDaddy*, rather than with your hosting company.

Nameservers connect ("point") your domain name - *yourawesomeblog.com* - to your hosted site.

If you purchased your domain through *InMotion* during sign up, you are good to go, no further steps needed.

If your domain is registered elsewhere, you need to point nameservers from the registrar to your hosting company.

Sounds complicated, but is really easy. Simply go to your registrar's account and click on:

Manage My Domains -> **Manage Domain Settings**
You will see something like the following screen:

Click on **Manage** (blue link) under **Nameservers** and insert the nameservers where you see them above:

NS1.INMOTIONHOSTING.COM
NS2.INMOTIONHOSTING.COM

That's it!

It can take from a few minutes to 24 hours to update, but *your* part is done.

Now that we got your blog all set up, you are ready to get creative and design your site.

Excited?

Step #4: WordPress Set Up

A first look at your site & features

Congratulations! - You have passed the technical steps of setting up your blog. Now it's time to get creative and design your site.

This will be fun......

When you installed Wordpress you were given a login link that ended with **/wp-admin**. Click on that now, and enter your user name and password.

This will get you into your Wordpress dashboard. Your Wordpress dashboard is different from your Inmotion dashboard which is only for your hosting *(you won't spend much there)*.

The Wordpress dashboard (or "backend") is where the magic happens, where you will design your site, enter content, etc.

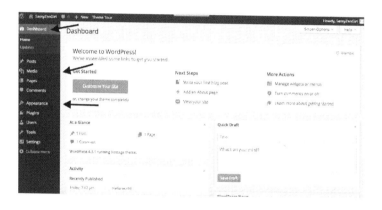

On the left, you will see a black vertical side bar with a number of options. At the top of that bar is **Dashboard**. Selecting this option will always get you back to your admin area from **Previews**, **Customize**, etc., so it's important to know where it's located.

Now, click on **My Blog** and then **Visit Site**. This will always give you the finished look of your site, as people will see it when they enter your url (minus the black *WordPress* bar at the top).

At the moment it looks very bleak, but that will soon change once we install a "theme" in the next chapter.

For now, let's just get an overview of the basic *WordPress* functions - without worrying about style and design.

Go back to:

My Blog (top left corner) -> **Dashboard**

and let's see what else we can find in the menu.

In the left menu bar, underneath the dashboard you will see **Posts**, **Media**, and **Pages**.

Pages vs Posts

Quite simply, "posts" are blog articles with time and date stamps, whereas pages are static (like a home page, about page, or contact page). You will probably use both in your blog, and they are customized in different areas within your *WordPress* admin board.

Try clicking on each, and you will see a few options coming up: **Add New**, **Categories**, etc. This is where you create and edit pages or posts.

To start a new page/post, simply click **Add New** and you will be led to a template that looks very similar to a word document with formatting options.

It is pretty self-explanatory and you can preview and update (=save) your page on the right.

Media

Here, you can upload pictures, video and audio. You can also upload media directly from the Page/Post Editor by selecting **Add Media**.

Appearance

This is the next menu option and will be one of the most important areas for designing your site. You can upload and customize your theme, create menus, edit widgets, and a number of other cool features.

The items in **Appearance** will vary slightly depending on the theme you choose, but most items are the same.

Plugins

"Plugins" are to *WordPress* what apps are to smart phones. We'll cover them in detail in *Step 6* but for now, just think of them as additional features like a contact page, facebook/twitter buttons, marketing tools, design features, etc. Whatever you could ever need, there will be a plugin for it.

Each theme already comes with a few plugins, and you can add as many as you like or need. Most are free and can be installed right from the *WordPress* plugin area. (explained in *Step 6*)

Users

This allows you to add additional users who have permission to modify your site, like a business partner, web designer, or tech support.

Settings

Additional customization features. All pretty self-explanatory. It's a good idea to look around the various options after you install your theme to get an overview of what is where. It may seem a lot at first, but once you use it a few times it will become easy and intuitive.

Congratulations! - You now have a basic understanding of how *WordPress* works.

In the next chapter we will put that knowledge to work and write your first post!

Step #5: Pick a Theme

Styling your site to awesomeness

Now that you have taken a first walk around your *WordPress* admin area, it is time to start designing your site and creating your first blog post.

Excited? - let's do it!

There are several options to find a good theme - both free and paid - depending on your needs.

First, let's clarify what a *THEME* is:

A theme is the "face" of your blog. It creates the overall design and style of your site as well as the individual page and post layout.

Think of a car: the *WordPress* software is what runs the site (like the engine, transmission, etc.). The theme provides the exterior (the body and trim of the car). This is what your visitors see when they come to your site.

When choosing a theme you have 3 options:

1) a *free theme*: can give you a basic start

2) a *low* to *medium priced premium theme* (ca. $10 - 40): most free themes can be upgraded to this option

3) an *advanced high priced premium theme* (ca. $60 - $150)

If you purchased the hosting package with **InMotion Hosting**, you already have access to a Premium Website Builder with 200+ Premium templates.

That will get you set up in no time with a professional looking blog/website.

Otherwise:

A good place to start is WordPress.org. They have a wide range of free themes, many with the option to upgrade to a premium version at a reasonable price.

For most new websites this option will be enough, at least to get you started.

You can try a free version and see if it's easy to use. If you like it, you upgrade to the premium version and gain access to more advanced features - which you will probably need eventually.

A lot of the higher priced themes are more complex, with lots of extra features that sound great, but can be confusing in the beginning. And sometimes you need "coding" (e.g., complex web designer lingo) to adjust them to your needs (even if the description claims that you don't!).

A simpler theme with not too much "schnick-schnack" is a good way to start and learn the basics of *WordPress*. Once you are more comfortable and feel there are additional features that you need, you can always upgrade. By then the learning curve will be a lot shorter.

Many features can be added with plugins (apps) and don't necessarily require a different theme - though there are certainly a number of good reasons to eventually upgrade once your site is growing. But then you will have a much better understanding of what you need, rather than being overwhelmed with a flood of new words and strange features that you have never heard of, let alone know how to use.

Eventually, you will want to switch to an advanced theme, because the features and overall functionality are amazing. But when you first start out, it's most important to get you going without too much frustration or a long learning curve.

If a theme is driving you crazy, change it! - It's not worth the aggravation and there are plenty of other themes that will serve your needs and are easy to use.

A great advantage of premium themes is tech support. Even as a beginner you might have specific needs or questions and having tech support will save you a lot of time.

Most themes though - even free themes - come with a "tour" to guide you through the basics and there are thousands of *Youtube* tutorials for any theme under the sun.

❀ ❀ ❀ ❀ ❀ ❀ ❀ ❀

To be honest, I found this whole process a little overwhelming in the beginning. A lot of the features were new to me and I didn't know what they meant.

If that doesn't scare you or you already found a theme that you like, feel free to skip to the next section. But if you would like a few pointers, I'll be happy to share:

I initially started on *Blogger/Blogspot* (remember, those "free" sites from Step 1.....?). It was a waste of time, and the constant limitations eventually forced me to move elsewhere.

After some rather frustrating experiences with more advanced themes that had dazzled me with amazing features but were much to complex for a beginner, I found an easy-to-use (and free) theme on WordPress and then upgraded to its Premium version since free themes are very limited.

Back then, **InMotion** didn't have the free website builder included yet, and certainly not the Premium builder they have now, or it would have been all much easier. Simple drag and drop, lots of professional functionality, perfect for a beginner with no experience. You have this option now, so that's where I would start if I had to do it over again:

Otherwise, just look through the "popular" free themes in your Wordpress backend (Appearances => Themes => Add new - see below) and pick one that already looks a lot like your desired result. Where you mostly have to change text and images, but not much else.

❊ ❊ ❊ ❊ ❊ ❊

If you want to add some more power, you can add **Thrive Architect** (*)

I call it my "Magic Wand"...;-) and used it to build my main site: SassyZenGirl.com

Thrive Architect is a Wordpress plugin that can be used with any theme and offers advanced design options that are incredibly easy to add. Just drag and drop, change colors and fonts - and your friends will think you hired an expensive designer...

The other amazing feature about *Thrive Architect* is that it comes with *Thrive Landing Pages*. Those are the pages you need to get people to sign up to your mailing list, **see here**:

Most providers will charge a monthly fee for the use of their landing page templates. The best known one - LeadPages - charges $25 per month! - With Thrive, it's a one time fee of $67 and you get lifetime access to all features, plus a large selection of pre-designed professionally looking landing pages. All you have to do is change text, colors and images and your website will look as though a professional designer had created it for you.

Do you need *Thrive*, just to get started? - Absolutely not! - But it's good to have as an option for later.

If you are brand new, don't worry too much about advanced features. The free Premium Website Builder from Inmotion Hosting will be all you need to get started with a great looking website, and once you know better what your specific needs are, you can always add *Thrive Content Builder* or upgrade to another theme.

Whatever you decide, it is important that you are comfortable with your theme, because it will be your daily companion for years to come and shouldn't be a constant frustration.

Installing your Theme

Now let's install your theme!

If you chose one from WorkPress.org, you can upload it directly from the *WordPress* admin area:

Simply go to:

Appearances -> **Themes**

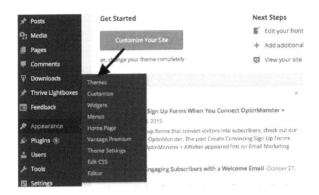

click **Add New**

enter the Theme name into the search bar on the right or find it by scrolling down the listings.

Hover over the Theme's image, click **Install** and when a new screen opens, click **Activate**.

That's it! - Your chosen theme is now running the show.

If you purchased a theme through another site, you were given a **download** link. The downloaded package will include a zip file and this is what you will upload to your *WordPress* account.

Appearances -> **Themes** -> **Add New** -> **Upload Theme** -> **Choose** the theme's zip file from your download folder -> **Activate Theme**

Once your theme is activated, **take a tour** to check out features and see where things are. Or just go through the options on the left side admin bar and click a few to get familiar. Most will be self-explanatory.

❄❄❄❄❄❄❄❄❄

As themes can vary greatly in structure and usability, we will only cover a few general basics here.

A good place to start is **Appearance**. You will find:

Theme Settings

Every theme will vary in options, but you always want to have **responsive** enabled in both layout and navigation. This ensures that your site looks good on any mobile device - phones, iPads, etc.

Customize

This option will take you to a different screen where you can customize the overall settings for your site: fonts, colors, header/footer styles, etc.

You can also set a **static front page** depending on your preferences. Static refers to a classic home page, like *luxurypetcompanion.com* vs. a blog page with changing blog posts, and date/time stamp as well as comments.

Home Page

This is usually the first page people see when they visit your site and a good place for a photo slider (=slide show). Sliders can be found at the bottom of the left admin menu, often called **Meta Slider**). Not every theme comes with a slider, but there are plugins you can add.

Menus

To set up a menu, select **Edit Menu** and then one of the options on the left side: **pages**, **posts**, etc. Once the tab opens select **Add to Menu** and fill in your menu titles, etc.

Widgets

Widgets are features that can be added in the side bars, header or footer. Things like a search bar, social media icons or an **About** section. Also an **Archive** or a list of most popular posts. There are many to choose from and this will be another fun (and easy) part of your design experience.

Pages & Posts

As covered earlier, there are two different areas to design **posts** and **pages**, because they function differently. Blog posts, for example, have time/date stamps and comment boxes. Both are found in the admin bar at the top left. Click on either and then **Add New**. From there, you can enter your text, media, etc. Now let's publish your first post!

Ready?

Publishing your first Post

Go to:

Posts -> Add New

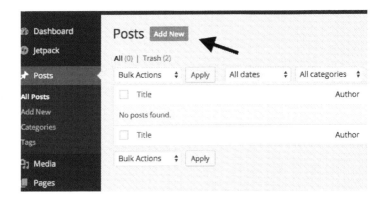

The following screen will open:

Enter a page title, something like "Welcome" or "My First Post", or whatever else comes to mind.

In the edit section, be sure you are on the **Visual** tab, not **Text**, and type something. Format any way you like, using the options at the top, very similar to *Microsoft Word*.

Now let's add a picture.

Click on:

Add Media -> **Select Files** -> find your picture and **upload** it -> **Insert into Post** at the bottom right.

You can also fill out the info on the right screen (title/caption, etc.)

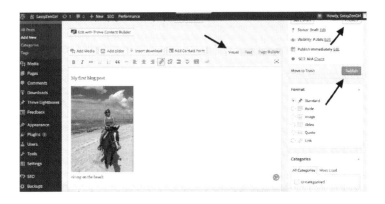

Next, click **Preview** in the upper right hand corner. The preview will open in a new window and you will see your first post in a basic design:

Close that window and click **Publish** on the upper right side.

Congratulations! - you have just published your first post.

❖❖❖❖❖❖❖❖

Next, you will want to change the design of your site and make it look more appealing. This will vary greatly with each theme, but the basic principles are always the same.

A good place to start is **Customize** (under *Appearances*) and set header/footer styles and colors, as well as font styles. This will also change the look of the individual pages and posts.

Next you might want to configure a **Menu** (also under *Appearances*). And then design each menu item under **Add Pages**. For a blog menu, use **Add Posts**. For the front page use **Home Page** (under *Appearances*).

These are some general pointers to get you started. The simpler themes are pretty intuitive and don't need much additional explanation beyond the steps given here.

If you still feel overwhelmed, a video tutorial is a great way to jump start your designing efforts. Most themes have video tutorials on their support page and also offer a start up tour right within the *WordPress* admin area.

YouTube offers tutorials for pretty much every theme under the sun. And *WordPress.org* and *WPBeginner.com* are additional great resources.

The most important thing will be not to get overwhelmed or stop altogether. Just take your time and go at your own pace.

Getting a basic site up and running is not that complicated and you can always add more features later. The more you work with *WordPress* - and your particular theme - the easier it will get. And eventually it will be really fun!

For now, we got your first post published!

Time to celebrate....

Step #6: Plugins, Mailing Lists & Google Analytics

Turning your blog into a Performance Ninja

Plugins

What the heck are "plugins"….?

Well…to make it simple, plugins are to *WordPress* what apps are to smartphones. They add cool features to the core *WordPress* software.

Some are essential, some are just fun, and we will cover both in this chapter.

There are thousands of *WordPress* plugins available, offering an abundance of options to customize your site. You will figure out what you need as you keep building and modifying your site, and it may change over time. There is a plugin for pretty much any feature you could ever need, but initially it is best to start with just a few. Too many active plugins can slow down the performance of your site and cause extended loading times for visitors.

Below is a list of 5 essential plugins that are widely used in the blogosphere, and I recommend you start with those. All of them are free (as most plugins are).

To install a plugin, simply go to **Plugins** (right underneath *Appearances*), click **Add New** and enter the name of the desired plugin in the search bar on the right.

Once your plugin comes up, click **Install Now**, wait a few seconds, and when a new screen appears click **Activate Plugin**.

That's all.

You can deactivate and reactivate plugins at any time by going to **Plugins** -> **Installed Plugins**.

Click on **Bulk Actions** and familiarize yourself with those options (also be found underneath each plugin).

If you downloaded a plugin to your hard drive - usually the case with paid plugins like *Thrive Architect* - click on **Upload Plugin** at the top of the **Add Plugin** window and continue from there.

7 Essential WordPress Plugins

Akismet

Blocks spam comments. *Really* important unless you enjoy cleaning up your "Comments" section every day.

Wordfence

A security plugin that protects your site from malware (viruses) and hacks.

W3 Total Cache

The most powerful performance plugin for *WordPress* sites. Dramatically improves the operational speed of your site.

WP-DBManager

An excellent choice to back up your site on a regular basis. You definitely want a backup plugin!

Smush

Automatically reduces the file size of your images without quality loss. This will greatly increase load time for your site as it won't take a minute for each image to load (you've seen those sites...)

Google Analyticator

see below

WordPress SEO by Yoast

"SEO"…..that word again!

If SEO (Search Engine Optimization) is new to you, don't worry, there will be more information in the final chapter.

Understanding SEO is really important, because it is the key ingredient for bringing more visitors to your site. It's what makes your site rank high in search engines like *Google* and *Bing*, so people can easily find you. Without proper SEO your site will get lost in cyberspace.

I takes time for SEO techniques to bear fruit and improve your ranking - at least a few months initially. That's why it's good to get started right away by at least adding some basic SEO info to your pages. That way your blog has time to build a web presence over time.

You don't need to understand all the ins and outs of SEO right now. But at least have it set up and put a title and a few keywords in to get you started (see *Step*

7 for more info). You can always modify them later once you had time to get more familiar with SEO, but don't ignore it completely, even if it may feel a lot right now.

You can also check out my Beginner SEO Book. Part 3 "On Page Optimization" is most important for you at this stage as it covers how to set up and structure your posts so google can find and rank them.

SassyZenGirl.com/SEO-Book

Yoast SEO is widely considered *THE* best tool to help you optimize your pages for search engine ranking. Provides feedback on your page/post content, pointing out things you might have forgotten or could improve. Also includes optimization for social media.

Easy to use and even offers a **tour** when you first open it:

Another important plugin is **Google XML Sitemaps.** This tool helps search engines analyze (= "crawl") your site to determine ranking. However, *Yoast SEO* includes **XML Sitemap** feature, so you can skip the google version.

5 more Awesome Plugins

The following plugins are helpful and widely used, but not essential in the beginning. If you feel overwhelmed, just skip to **Google Analytics** *for now. Otherwise, read on for some more cool WordPress apps:*

SumoMe

A popular (and free) floating **social media sharebar.** "Floating" means the sharebar stays with the reader as they are scrolling down the text. This plugin comes with a lot of other cool features - all free - and it looks pleasant.

Contact Form 7

If your theme doesn't come with a contact form, this plugin is the most widely used option with over 9 million downloads. It includes *CAPTCHA*, *Askimet* spam filtering, and multiple templates that can be customized to your needs.

Click to Tweet

Allows you to place a "click to tweet" button next to a quote inside a blog post.

Pretty Link

Allows you to create "pretty links" that include your website name and are easy to remember. For example, if I wanted to link out to this book, rather then giving out the Amazon url, which is impossible to remember:

https://www.amazon.com/dp/B07JCJC45L/

I can use pretty link and turn that into:

SassyZenGirl.com/Start-A-Blog
or
SassyZenGirl.com/BlogBook or similar.

Duplicate Post

Allows you to clone a page, if you want to reuse the layout or design.

Google Analytics (GA)

The most important tool for analyzing and tracking your blog traffic will be *Google Analytics*. It is the industry standard for website analytics and an absolute must.

Google Analytics helps you to assess how well pages, posts and features are doing, where to best place a newsletter sign-up, or how to improve search engine ranking.

If you ever want to work with advertisers, PR agencies or sponsors, they will want statistics pulled from *Google Analytics*, so it is important to get it set up from the start.

Even if you are not planning to monetize your site, it will still be an important tool to help you measure what works and what doesn't, and how to grow your audience.

If this feels overwhelming, don't worry, you don't have to apply it all right away.

I will help you set up your *GA* account, and then you can leave it for a while and focus on other things - like designing your site and writing cool posts.

There are many excellent articles on how to best use *Google Analytics,* and in good time you will want to read some of them. For now, though, let's just get you set up and have that out of the way.

Setting Up Google Analytics

Go to *analytics.google.com* and sign up by following the prompts. If you don't have a Google account yet (e.g., through a gmail address) you will be asked to create one, but you can use your regular email address (doesn't have to be gmail).

Next, you will be guided to this screen for ***Google Analytics*** **sign up**:

Click **Sign up** and on the next screen follow the prompts:

Account: This will be the "umbrella name" for your GA account. You can have several different websites under one account, but this is the overall name. You can use your blog's name or any other name.

Property: Enter your website name and url.

Scroll down and click, **Get tracking ID**.

Next, you will see some code - no need to panic…;-) - just hang in there…

First, go to

Admin -> **Property Settings** -> turn on each of the tabs under **Advertising Features**. This will give you additional data from each visitor. These need to be turned on from the start to deliver accurate data.

Now back to the code. Thankfully, there is a great plugin that will place the code for you, making things very easy:

Google Analyticator

If you haven't already installed and activated this plugin, do it now, and then click on the **Google Analytics** tab in the left *WordPress* Admin bar.

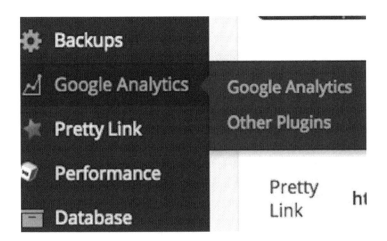

This will lead you to **Basic Settings**. Make sure that **Google Analytics logging** is **enabled**, and select the correct **Analytics Account**. Then press **Save**.

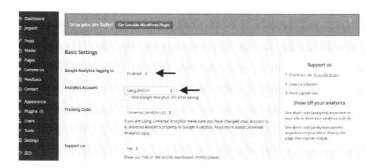

Next, you will see a message in your dashboard: *"Don't miss your crawl errors: connect with Google Search Console here."*

Click on the link, then click on **Get Google Authorization Code**.

In the pop-up, click **Allow**, and then copy and paste the prompted code into the box. Then click **Authenticate** and **Save Profile**.

All done!

Seeing Your First Statistics

Google updates data several times a day. Go to **Reporting** and try the various options in the left hand sidebar. To see who is on your site right now, click **Real time -> Overview**.

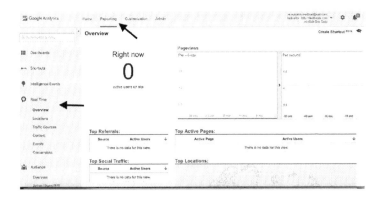

Of course, you won't see anything right after set-up, so give it a day, or at least a few hours, and then check again.

As your site grows, this will be really fun and also give you valuable insight for improving your site.

Mailing List & Email Marketing Services

The final tool we will explore in this chapter are mailing list services. This is where email addresses go when someone signs up to your newsletter.

These services provide sign up forms as well as landing pages like "please confirm your subscription" and so on.

They also manage your email campaigns and help you schedule automated responders or an email series. And they will send out your newsletters.

As usual, there are many options to choose from, but the following two are the most widely used among bloggers:

1) **AWeber**

2) **MailChimp**

Unlike most services described in this guide, switching mailing list companies is not without challenges.

The main problem is that ALL your subscribers have to resubscribe when you switch to a new service.

To clarify: yes, your new mailing list service can import your subscriber list, but they are still required by law to ask every subscriber to opt in again. Otherwise, they would be spamming them.

Naturally, not every subscriber will do it - some simply forget or are too busy - and you will loose quite a few.

Therefore, it is really important to pick the "right" service for your needs from the start and most bloggers use *AWeber*.
MailChimp starts with a free version up to a certain subscriber number, but has some limitations when it comes to auto-responder campaigns. And it's not as user friendly as *AWeber*.

This video shows you how to set up a sign up to mailing list sequence with landing page, thank you page and download page. It seems very complicated when you do it for the first time, but this video should make it very easy to set up. This is a sequence from landing page to mailing list.

VIDEO: Setting up a Sign up Sequence from Landing Page to Mailing List

SassyZenGirl.com/Mailing-List-Sequence

You can use the same process when setting up sign up forms in your side bar. In that case, you can pick a free plugin like **Optin Cat**, create a form and then connect it to your mailing list provider just as shown in this video.

SassyZenGirl Blogging Bootcamp
(Special Limited Time 50% Discount)

Based on the questions and feedback I received from my readers around the world, I recently released a Course for Beginner Bloggers - *SassyZenGirl's Blogging Bootcamp* - that takes what I teach in this book a big step further with easy-to-follow, over-the-shoulder video introductions on all the technical steps of starting a successful blog, plus:

- *Monetization*
- *Blog Style Writing*
- *SEO (=Google Optimization)*
- *Setting up Sign up Forms & Mailing Lists*

27 Video Lessons, available online 24/7. You go at your own pace. Lifetime access, incl. all updates.

Normally, this course sells for $97, but for a limited time, you can get a 50% discount using this link and only pay $47:

SassyBlogBootcamp.com

Step #7: Blogging & Marketing Training

Learning from the Masters

There are millions of blogs in the blogosphere (love that word…;-), but many are "ghost towns" with few if any subscribers. The problem is usually not the content quality, but rather a lack of understanding of how successful blogging works - both on the writing and the marketing side.

To be a successful blogger takes a variety of skills:

- *Improving your writing/blogging style*
- *Finding content that is trending*
- *Search engine ranking (SEO)*
- *Generating traffic and building a subscriber list*
- *Social media marketing*
- *Finding your niche*

and much more.

Below is a list of top resources to help you in your blogging career. Most of it them are free and come from the top bloggers in the world, sharing their tips and insights.

Studying even a few will save you a LOT of time and frustration and will also connect you with other bloggers in your field.

There are a lot of simple things you can do that will greatly enhance your chances of being successful, and these are the guys to learn from. They are the best of the best, some of the biggest, most successful bloggers and online marketers in the world, and they offer a TON of free information, courses and eBooks that will save you time, and help you get started the right way.

If you want to be successful, make your voice heard AND make money along the way: learn from the best!

So here we go:

*Refining your writing skills

- **Jon Morrow's Course** - The best blog-style writing course available and covers <u>much</u> more than just writing: *SassyZenGirl.com/Guest-Blogging*

- **EnchantingMarketing.com** - excellent tips for brilliant online & copywriting delivered in "snackable" form….

*How to draw traffic to your site

- **Guest Blogging** - Writing guest articles for well known blogs is one of *THE* most effective strategies to build a following for your blog. John Morrow's course I mentioned above is the best course around and the link will get you a 30% discount! Includes a "Black Book" with editor's emails for some of the highest ranked blogs on the internet (incl. Forbes, Huffington Post and Lifehacker) - This is a paid course, but WELL worth it!!

- **This course shares** how 2 bloggers generate 100K PER MONTH from 2 blogs. They started generating 20K after 9 months using this method and now, 3 years, later are at a 100K per month - really! (not a scam, just smart marketing).

SassyZenGirl.com/Pinterest-Course

- **Free 5-Part Mini Video Series** on the 5 most powerful traffic sources today.

  SassyZenGirl.com/Traffic-Bonanza

- **My little SEO Beginner Guide** *(see below)*

- **BackLinko.com** - awesome and very unique tips on SEO and link building

*Monetize your Blog

- **Affiliate Marketing** - How this blogger earns 50K per month!

  SassyZenGirl.com/Affiliate-Course

- **6 Figure Blogger:**

  SassyZenGirl.com/6-Figure-Blogger

*Become a successful Travel Blogger

- **Top Rate Travel Blogging Course** - From one of the most successful travel bloggers in the world: Nomadic Matt. If anyone can show you how to crush it as a travel blogger, it's Matt!

  SassyZenGirl.com/Travel-Blogger

The next books in the *SassyZenGirl* Series **will go in-depth** into growing an audience:

* choosing a blog topic that works
* the writing style of blogging
* how to drive traffic to your blog!
* how to monetize your blog

#3-5 cover additional methods of traffic generation:

#3 - SEO (How to rank in Google)

a MUST for every blogger or website owner
Understanding SEO is the foundation for everything else and will change
* how you structure your site and
* how you write your posts!

#4 - Social Media Marketing

Winning Strategies for Quickly
Growing a Following on:
Youtube
Instagram
Pinterest
Twitter
Facebook

Kindle Bestseller Publishing

One of the easiest and fastest ways
to grow a following
for your blog, business & social networks
while establishing yourself
as an authority in your field

FREE Bonus Masterclass

As a special bonus to my readers, I created this **FREE Masterclass** outlining *the exact strategies* I used to build a 6 Figure Passive Income Business and the Financial Freedom that allows me to travel the world while running my business from a laptop - mostly on autopilot.

Are you ready for a change?

Special Masterclass
100K BESTSELLER BLUEPRINT:

The *Proven Step-by-Step System* To Grow A
6 Figure Business from Bestseller Publishing &
Massively Explode Your Existing Business As A
#1 Bestselling Author!

*…Even if you are **not a Writer** - have **no Following** and **NO CLUE about Marketing!***

Register here:
100KBestseller.com

What you will learn in this all new Training:

*SECRET #1: *Why 99% of Self-published authors fail + how YOU can become a member of the exclusive 1% Club - even after all the recent Amazon changes.*

*SECRET #2: *The 4-Week Plan to your first #1 Bestseller!*

*SECRET #3: *How to turn your books into a 6 Figure Passive Income Machine - completely on Autopilot - over the next 6-12 Months.*

Register here:
100KBestseller.com

See ya at the class… :)

Final Words

You made it to the end - *Congratulations!*

I hope you are happy with the results and enjoy building your blog. You now have a clear roadmap and can start rockin' in cyberspace.

Blogging is an exciting journey, and while there will be ups and downs as with any path worth taking, if you keep at it and keep improving your skills, the sky will be the limit.

If you feel a little overwhelmed from time to time, just go slowly, step by step, maybe 30 min per day, and within a short time you will be amazed at what you have achieved.

Steady does it, and if you are passionate about all the wonderful things you have to share with the world, a brief technical learning curve will not stop you!

If you need support, want to network with other new bloggers or just ask a question, come join us in the *SassyZenGirl Facebook Networking & Support Group:*

SassyZenGirl.Group

a thriving new community of newbie bloggers, authors and entrepreneurs. You can also share your new blog there and get feedback.

Once the technical set up of your blog is completed, this book will show you how to attract an audience and monetize your blog. It's the next book in the blogging series:

Or...if you want to take it a step further - **INFLUENCER FAST TRACK**, my newest book, will show you everything you need to know - A to Z, step by step:

I wish you all the best and much success on this new adventure. Don't forget to have fun along the way! You will grow your audience a lot faster if you enjoy what you do..;-)

Finally - if you enjoyed this book, it would be **AWEsome** if you could

leave a quick review on Amazon.

It only takes a minute and would mean a LOT!!
You can also share this pink baby on Goodreads if that's one of your digs...:) - Thank you so very much - YOU ROCK!!

Wishing you all the very best - always!

Gundi Gabrielle aka SassyZenGirl

More SassyZenGirl Yummies

COURSES

SassyZenGirl's Blogging Bootcamp
SassyBlogBootcamp.com

FREE Masterclass:
POWER MARKETING BLUEPRINT
100KBestseller.com

Award Winning
INFLUENCER FAST TRACK
Series

#1 Bestselling
BEGINNER INTERNET MARKETING
Series
"The Sassy Way... when you have NO CLUE!"

#1 Bestselling
TRAVEL BOOKS

Score FREE Flights, Rental
Cars & Accommodations.
Dramatically reduce Airfares.
Get paid to Travel & START a
DIGITAL NOMAD BIZ
you can run from anywhere
in the world!

ZEN TRAVELLER
BALI
A QUICK GUIDE

Explore the "real" Bali…
The quiet, magical parts
far away from the
tourist crowds…

About the Author

Gundi Gabrielle, aka *SassyZenGirl*, loves to explain complex matters in an easy to understand, fun way. Her *"The Sassy Way...when you have NO CLUE!!"* series has helped thousands around the world conquer the jungles of internet marketing with humor, simplicity and some sass.

A 11-time #1 Bestselling Author, Entrepreneur and former Carnegie Hall conductor, Gundi employs marketing chops from all walks of life and loves to help her readers achieve their dreams in a practical, fun way. Her students have published multiple #1 Bestsellers outranking the likes of Tim Ferris, John Grisham, Hal Elrod and Liz Gilbert.

When she is not writing books or enjoying a cat on her lap (or both), she is passionate about exploring the world as a Digital Nomad, one awesome adventure at a time.

She has no plans of settling down anytime soon.

SassyZenGirl.com
SassyZenGirl.Group
DreamClientsOnAutopilot.com

Instagram.com/SassyZenGirl
Youtube.com/c/SassyZenGirl
Facebook.com/SassyZenGirl
Twitter.com/SassyZenGirl

Made in the USA
Middletown, DE
03 May 2019